THE LITTLE BOOK OF

POCKET SPELLS

The Little Book of
Pocket
Spells

Akasha Moon

RIDER
LONDON · SYDNEY · AUCKLAND · JOHANNESBURG

Published in 2001 by Rider, an imprint of Ebury Publishing

Ebury Publishing is a Random House Group company

Copyright © Akasha Moon 2001

The Random House Group Limited Reg. No. 954009

Addresses for companies within the Random House Group can be found at
www.randomhouse.co.uk

A CIP catalogue record for this book is available from the British Library

Printed and bound in India by Gopsons Papers Ltd

ISBN 9780712614191

Copies are available at special rates for bulk orders. Contact the sales
development team on 020 7840 8487 for more information.

To buy books by your favourite authors and register for offers, visit
www.randomhouse.co.uk

The Random House Group Limited supports the Forest Stewardship
Council® (FSC®), the leading international forest-certification
organisation. Our books carrying the FSC label are printed on
FSC®-certified paper. FSC is the only forest-certification scheme
supported by the leading environmental organisations, including
Greenpeace. Our paper procurement policy can be found at
www.randomhouse.co.uk/environment

MAGICK NAME

Create a magickal persona for yourself by choosing a name that inspires you. It is common practice in magick and spellcraft to use ancient, powerful appellations. They attract concomitant energies (so pick carefully!) and assist in elevating the practitioner from mundane associations. Goddess-names work well, with perhaps an appending phrase that sums up your associations. An intuitive person with a love of ancient Egypt, who enjoys self-expression through movement, and who has additional fiery affiliations might call herself 'Isis Firedancer', for example.

THE WHEEL OF LIFE

Witches and magickians ride the tide of the seasons and employ the dates of the ancient festivities for particular purposes, as follows:

* Samhain (31October): to access and process issues from the past; also for divination, purification.

* Winter Solstice/Yule (21 December): to celebrate and nurture the life force, take stock and make long-term plans.

* Imbolc (2 February): to welcome the oncoming light born of the winter darkness.

* Spring Equinox (21 March): for boundless energy; for facilitating a complete change in your life.

* Beltane (1 May): for energy, new ideas and sexuality.

* Summer Solstice (21 June): for relating the mystical to the physical; enlightenment, working on new levels.

* Lammas/Lughnasadh (1 August): for celebrating the harvest of past efforts, reflecting on industry, replenishment.

* Mabon/Autumn Equinox (21 September): for temperance, stoicism, balance, altering tides of fortune.

AURIC FACIAL

The aura is the energy-field that surrounds every object. Our individual auras influence and are influenced by the body.

To give yourself an auric facelift that diminishes wrinkles on this plane, rub your hands together, palm to palm, then separate them, palms facing one another. Move your hands together and apart a little. You should feel your aura's energy building up. Now, with light, upward movements, keeping your hands about two inches from your face (or however far you wish yet without losing the energy), stroke your face's aura. It is rather like slowly splashing your face with water. Repeat as often as you like. Daily is best.

VISUALISATION FOR EFFERVESCENCE

If you are feeling lack-lustre but need to be the life and soul, or at least to entertain, imagine that your aura is made out of pink champagne. Watch it weave and bubble about all those around you, the most decadent of Jacuzzis in which all become enlivened, their own auras tingling in response. Done properly, this visualisation is guaranteed to tickle the fancies of all concerned, and give rise to a sparkling and fun-filled event.

LUNAR TIDES

Every lunar cycle is an opportunity
to implement change, culminating in
the celebration of the full moon.
Phases should be employed
sympathetically, as follows:

*New moon — initiating or
augmenting projects, practical
endeavours

*Waxing moon — to develop
ideas and spells. Daily and
with a view is the moon is
best. As the moon waxes, so
too do your fortunes

*Full moon — to bring a cycle of
growth to fruition, and to give
thanks

- ★Waning moon — to corrode negative influences

- ★Dark moon — destruction of obstacles, turning negatives into creativity, self-exploration

ENCOURAGING WEALTH

For prosperity, add silver coins to your bath when the moon is waxing. As you splash around, envisage yourself with enough material wealth to allow you to enjoy life and express your potential to the full.

RIDING THE TIDES

In the Western hemisphere, seasonal tides may be employed as follows:

* 21 December–21 March: getting rid of what is obsolete in your life, forming solid foundations.

* 21 March–21June: setting plans into action, initiating new schemes.

* 21 June–21 September: developing ideas, enjoying the fruits of past labour.

* 21 September–21 December: taking stock of patterns of progress to date; formulating, innovating.

CANDLE MAGICK

Candles may be used to facilitate many types of magick. Colours are significant, both traditionally and personally, helping to create a conducive mood. A few examples of the colours and their usage are:

* Blue, for calm, and study

* Red, for love and passion

* Pink, for fun, compassion

* Green, for new beginnings and initiating projects

* Yellow, for wealth, health and happiness

PURIFICATION BATH

Had an unpleasant experience? A handful of salt in the bath-water will cleanse you. Visualise it glowing blue-white and, as you enter the water, 'see' your astral body being purified. At the end, envisage the negative effects of the experience spiralling away down the plug-hole.

ALL-PURPOSE MAGICKAL CIRCLE

A Circle brings enhanced spiritual experience and instant protection. To cast one anywhere, even on the bus to work, all you have to know is which direction you are facing. With yourself at the centre, visualise to the

* East: yellow light, Air

* South: red light, Fire

* West: blue light, Water

* North: green light, Earth

Imagine all negativity bouncing off the outside of your sphere, and your mind now free to connect with uncontaminated, higher realms.

FOCUSING
CANDLE MAGICK

To 'magnetise' a candle, dip your
thumb and forefinger in an oil
relevant to your cause, or in an all-
purpose 'magnetising oil', and rub
from the centre of the candle's stem
to the tip, then from the centre to
the base, many times, envisaging
the purpose of your spell being
realised as you do so.

SIMPLE SPELL
FOR LOVE

To entrance another, work on the first
Friday of a new moon. Write their full
name in red ink on a piece of paper,
and burn it in the flame of a red
magnetised candle (use tweezers!)

Now say:

*'[Their full name], if you be
free and willing, come thee to
me, the living embodiment of
Aphrodite.'*

(If you are male, say:

*'As the living embodiment
of Aphrodite.'*)

Repeat at the same time every
Friday until the moon is full.

WORDS OF POWER

The words used in a spell are of the utmost importance. Some witches and magickians use specific alphabets such as Enochian (created by Dr John Dee, the Elizabethan astrologer, and said to be 'the language of Angels'), to enhance their work. Often, written spells are translated into runes or other scripts. The concentration involved helps imprint the intent on the subconscious.

Simplicity is of the essence in magick. Words should be chosen with care; it is always important to avoid ambivalence in spellcraft.

Naïve rhymes have a stronger effect
than complex ritual incantations,
and repetition during visualisation
is a key to success.

At the end of clearly stating an aim,
the witch adds: 'An' it harm none.
So mote it be!' Better no result than
the creation of bad repercussions,
which are believed in Wicca to
return threefold.

OM

Om, or *Aum*, is one of the simplest and most magickal doorways in existence. Try meditating on it, vibrating it throughout your body. It empowers, cleanses and intensifies spiritual aspiration. *Om* is literally a gateway between worlds. Frequent practice and concentration will bring remarkable results.

THE ETHICS

*An' it Harm None,
Do What Thou Wilt*

(The Wiccan Rede)

I CAN'T BELIEVE IT'S MONDAY AGAIN!

Monday is, of course, sacred to the moon. Despite the hassle of another working week, the witch finds time to optimise on the planetary influence most pertinent to witchcraft. Purification, psychism, magickal enhancement and healing spells are all performed on Mondays. Of course, the phase of the moon is also significant. Corresponding incenses and oils include chamomile, eucalyptus, jasmine and lemon. Candles should be silver, white or indigo.

MARTIAN CONTACT

Tuesday is ruled by Mars, which makes it the right day for spells for strength, courage, facing challenges and overcoming obstacles. Oils used in such workings include ginger, High John the Conqueror and basil. Colours for candles are red and deep orange.

WORDS ABOUT WEDNESDAY

As Wednesday is ruled by Mercury, the emphasis is on communication, swiftness, precision, transport and travel, and study. Concentration and accuracy should be produced by a spell or meditation performed on this day, so it's perfect for intellectual work or magickal pursuits concerning words, magickal alphabets and teaching. It is also relevant to computing, now the main medium of many witches! Lily of the valley, lemon grass, and clover are all suitable scents or oils. Candles should be yellow.

JOVIAL INFLUENCES

To induce friendship, companionship, to aid family concord and to bring luck and prosperity, work on a Thursday. Suitable oils and incenses include clove, honeysuckle, nutmeg and sage. Colours include gold, green and royal purple. Jupiter's influence brings generosity and warmth to any magickal procedures, and is beneficial to any project involving 'expansion'.

THANK THE GODDESS IT'S FRIDAY

As well as bringing the working week to a close, Venus' day graces us with delicious celestial influences.

Friday is the day to cast spells for love, beauty, friendship and passion. Candles should be green, red or pink, and the mood sensual, the scents musky, flowery or fruity, such as frangipani, rose or raspberry.

A long soak in a magickal bath surrounded by candles will bring extra happiness and beneficial influences to your workings.

SATURDAY'S SPELLS

Use Saturn's day to aid work within a partcular structure or hierarchy. Though most people use it simply to shop and relax, Saturday will bring rewards to those who apply themselves on it. Career, property and ambition are highlighted, so magick and mental effort will pay off. It is also good for casting banishing spells. Cypress and patchouli are amongst the scents appropriate to Saturn; candles should be purple, black, white or green, depending on your purpose.

SUNDAY SPELLS
SPIRITUALITY

The seventh day is the ideal time
to tune in to the spiritual and
mystical side of your nature.
Burning frankincense, and gold and
orange candles, will help attune you
to the wealth of spiritual knowledge
waiting to harmonise your life.
This is also a propitious time for
healing and creative work.

TO LIFT THE BLUES

Orange oil is powerfully uplifting.
Evaporating some, or using a few
drops in the bath, will help dissipate
the blues. For added clout, use an
orange candle in conjunction.
Several of them placed around the
bath as you soak will lift
your spirits.

If in more ritualistic mode, place six
of them about the room so that you
stand in a circle of light.

Imagine an equilateral cross at your
solar plexus. If it seems to waver or
be imbalanced, invest energy into
keeping it still and upright. (This
cross represents your 'centredness'
in the Universe).

Finally, imagine a stream of orange-yellow light pouring into you. The candle flames are foci for this force. Wrap the light of the flames around yourself until you are 'cloaked' in an astral raiment.

Return to your workaday life as a rejuvenated Child of Light.

REJUVINATION BATH

This works best using a real emerald, so buy or borrow one for the best effect.

Put the emerald in the bath (make sure the plug is in!) in about five inches of lukewarm / cold water. Allow to soak for at least one hour. Remove the emerald, and add warm / hot water. Sprinkle with seven drops of either basil, thyme or lavender essential oils (if pregnant, use a dilute form, such as scented bath bubbles).

When immersed, rest the emerald on your sternum, at the heart chakra (one of the seven major energy points of the body and aura).

Envisage its brilliant green rejuvination energy permeating the water, and you. Do not arise until every cell in your body has been aurically saturated in this way.

INCENSE TIP

Loose incenses are perfect accompaniments to spells, allowing you to carefully select the right herbs, gums and woods according to their correspondences. However, the charcoal discs on which they are burned often spit and create a terrible smog. To avoid this, light the disc and leave to smoulder somewhere safe for twenty minutes before sprinkling the incense.

WATERFRONT SPELL 1

To bring rewarding adventures into
your life, find a fallen twig that
appeals to you. You can correspond
the wood to your aim by deciding
which planet is appropriate to your
intent (Jupiter, for prosperity and
expansion, for example), and finding
a tree ruled by it. (Nutmeg is one
such for Jupiter.) It is best not to
take it directly from the tree, but if
you have no choice, be modest, and
say 'please' and 'thank you' to the
Dryad, the spirit of the tree.

Whittle your small twig into a
wand whilst concentrating on the
adventures and rewards you
wish for.

On the day of a new moon, take the magick wand to a river or the sea (never an enclosed body of water such a lake!), concentrate hard on what you wish for, stating it out loud if desired/possible, and throw it as far out as you can manage. Visualise the energies you have sent flowing out into the universe, to return, eventually, laden with exotic possibilities.

WATERFRONT SPELL 2

To rid yourself of unwanted energies, take a handful of soil and concentrate into it thoughts of what you wish to shed.

When you are satisfied that your thoughts have imbued the soil, place in a permeable pouch such as cheesecloth and, as you tie it, visualise these undesirable influences as now being cut off from your life.

When the moon is waning or dark, take it (during the day is fine) to an open waterfront, and hurl it in. As the water saturates it, it is cleansed, and as it is carried away from you, so are the unwanted influences removed from your life.

BATHTIME BREW

Herbs in the bath will imbue you with their special properties, and make the steam refreshing and cleansing. Experiment with different shrubs and combinations.

Favourites include:

* Rosemary for confidence

* Thyme for creativity and strength in your own convictions

* Lavender to refresh and brace

* Sage for love, cleanliness, for dispelling infections such as colds, and stimulation

(NB: Herbs should always be used with caution, especially when pregnant.)

GRIS GRIS

If somebody is giving you grief, either magickally or psychologically, you can shield yourself from their influence with the following technique.

Write their name in black at the centre of a thick piece of paper.

Fold it up, starting by creasing it across their name.

Keep folding, imagining their power diminishing, until you have the smallest possible capsule of paper. Now burn it somewhere from which you can later retrieve the ash, saying:

'Your power is dying; I cancel thee out. [Their name], I cancel thee out,'

repeating as many times as required to facilitate a strong mental image of you doing just this.

When all the embers have died, carefully collect the remains, and store in a black silk scarf or pouch, preferably with a sample of their hair, or some nail clippings.

This mixture can be used as a base for further antidote processes.

ANTIDOTE 1

The best antidote in the world is to ignore your aggressor — and literally not give them a second thought. Antipathy builds up very strong links.

If these links are already established, one way to diminish them is to take a salt bath. Whilst in soak, imagine the chords which connect you and 'X' dissolving in the bright, cleansing light of the salt water.

When you emerge from the bath, pull the plug, and as the water drains from the tub, sprinkle in the ash produced in the 'gris gris' spell (see p.36), and visualise it effervescing white light and dissolving. Then watch it go down the plug-hole on this plane. Make sure none of it remains in the bath.

This simple technique works for many problems, as it eliminates unwanted influences. Performing it with the waning or dark moons will help for 'ridding', or the new moon for new beginnings and growing inner strength.

ANTIDOTE 2

Take a pinch of the ash from the 'gris gris' process on p.36, and mix with some banishing (or cleansing) oil. Take a black candle and anoint it from centre to both ends, mentally imbuing it with your feelings of antipathy for the other person concerned. When the moon is just beginning to wane, light it. As the wax melts down, so will their hostile influence on you. Repeat daily until the dark moon.

CURE FOR FORGETFULNESS

Drunk daily, this simple potion will help revive flagging brain cells. Take a large pinch of dried rosemary, and the same of dried sage. Add boiling water and steep for at least five minutes. If you remember to drink this as often as possible, you're on your way!

ANTIDOTE 3

If you are faced with a persistent problem person, try the following. Take the rest of the 'gris-gris' ash (or make more, which you may need to do if you have already worked the spells above — see p.36), and, by the light of a waning moon, and working on a Saturday, mix with a little St John's wort. This herb is active against evil, and helps to protect and purify.

Standing over the mixture, chant: 'By the power of Saturn, I cast thee out!' — strongly envisaging your aggressor losing their grip on your psyche and well-being.

If the person is particularly tenacious, you might like to burn the resultant mixture in a ritual of your own device (always the best sort). Each cleansing by fire will loosen their influence.

Then, wear a little St John's wort in a pouch about your neck.

Alternately, wear the entire original mixture about your person, in a pouch.

ASTRAL
AIR FRESHNER 1

Garlic has a reputation for banishing vampires (though most vampires I know love garlic!). However, it does absorb negative energy, so, if there are bad vibes in your house, leaving peeled cloves of garlic, slightly nicked, about the place will help. These must be removed or replaced every twenty-four hours.

ASTRAL
AIR FRESHNER 2

This may pong a little on the material planes, but has been used for centuries to clear negative energies. Simply, place a cut onion in the vicinity that needs cleansing. The evil influences will be drawn to it and get caught in its numerous layers. Throw it out and replace, if necessary, every twenty-four hours.

SLEEP WELL

To ensure that a dear departed is 'asleep' to this realm (i.e. is progressing spiritually, rather than being caught up with the trivial/emotional issues of their last life), light a small white candle (preferably on the anniversary of their death), and burn a little lad's love as you work.

Meditate on the fact that emotional and spiritual bonds endure, but that specific circumstances change. Send your love to the soul concerned, perhaps with a few words of peaceful encouragement. Do not be selfish and hold them back with sentiment. Imagine them liberated from all worldly concerns.

Now envisage a thick curtain
descending between you both. That
is the way it should be, for now. Let
the incense out of the window and
extinguish the candle.

MARITAL BLISS

A crystal bowl containing rosewater,
on which seven drops of essential
rose oil are placed, will keep a
marriage sweet. Place it in the
bedroom. If it needs a boost, add
fresh rose petals. However, never
allow the petals to decay.
The fresher the water, the more
blissful the union.

ALL NIGHT LONG

The aphrodisiac has to be one of the world's most-used enchantments. There are literally thousands available, and all cultures have them. The following is a relatively gentle spell!

Take a teaspoon of cinnamon, and add to it seven drops of essential rose oil. Boil up a small pan of lovage leaves (dried lovage is fine) for five minutes. Leave to steep for another two. Add one tablespoon of this to the previous ingredients (use the spare lovage potion for your pre-all night bath!). As you do so, contemplate the pleasures you intend to enjoy.

Leave the mixture out to dry —
beneath the sun is best. Finally,
when the mixture has returned to
powder, sprinkle it lightly on the bed
you wish to bless.

BLESSING FOOD

For real nourishment on every
plane, psychically enhance your
food by holding your hands over it
and mentally (or verbally, if at
home) reciting a small prayer or
mantra of thankfulness. As you do
so, visualise positive energy pouring
from the Universe into your hands,
and then being directed into
the food before you.

ARABIAN NIGHTS

This spell is best performed on a Friday.

To attract as many friends and lovers as your heart desires, take nine drops from a phial of jasmine oil, preferably with some real jasmine or lilac flowers in the bowl, and add to it a spoonful of rosewater.

Stand with your hands over the sweet-smelling combination, and concentrate pink light into the bowl. See the potion glowing with attractive, fun energies.

Dab a little behind your ears and on your wrists before you go out.

Be aware of the pink light,
concentrated at your pulse-points,
colouring your entire aura.
Now, enjoy!

ASTRAL TRAVEL

To facilitate astral travel, envisage
yourself, when on the verge of
sleep, travelling towards a huge
silver-white moon set in an indigo
sky. As you drift off, try to pass into
the orb — and beyond it. Burning a
little jasmine incense, or placing a
(preferably silver or indigo) cloth
with nine drops of the oil on it under
your pillow will also aid astral
projection.

FAST GOOD LUCK

The Wheel of Fortune is always turning. Every individual receives their quota of circumstances, both good and bad, throughout the course of their incarnations. If you are undergoing a run of bad luck, it is because there is something you need to learn — an attitude perhaps, which needs to be processed, or the effect of actions passed which needs to be nullified (usually involving some discomfort).

However, the key point in all of these issues is to strive.

To encourage the Wheel of Fortune to carry you upward again, visualise yourself on the Wheel, at whatever point you believe yourself to be. With all the mental and spiritual energy you can muster, make the Wheel rotate so that it carries you skyward. Be sure to do this clockwise, or you will take a dip before you ascend! Repeat daily until luck is working in your favour again.

LUCKY LODESTONE

Clove oil is renowned for attracting power and good luck. However, it is rather irritating to the skin, so, rather than wearing it, anoint a small magnet, whilst beseeching the gods to look upon you kindly. The most relevant to this spell is Hermes, who brought sudden windfalls to the ancient Greeks. The Hindu goddess Laksmi is also connected with prosperity and good luck. Use a deity you feel a rapport with. When you receive inner acknowledgement that your request has been granted, wrap the magnet in bright yellow silk and carry it with you at all times. The unexpected should become a delight after this!

CONCENTRATION

Rosemary is renowned in herbal lore
as a concentration aid. Whilst
working, evaporate the oil to keep
yourself focussed. Dried leaves can
also be steeped in boiling water and
drunk as tea. My personal favourite
is to keep a rosemary plant close to
where you work. A gentle rub of the
leaves releases a magickal,
refreshing fragrance ideal to help
you focus.

TO KEEP YOUR LOVER
FAITHFUL

Take a small, unwashed garment
that belongs to your partner. Hold
it, and contemplate your intimacy,
the sacredness of your union
(despite the grubby garment!) and
the shared times to come.

Place it before you, take some
wintergreen oil, and, whilst looking
at the latter, mentally block out all
potential assailants of your
partnership. See barriers come down
between your lover and any
interlopers.

Lightly sprinkle the garment with
your oil, saying :

*'Be it night or be it day,
You shall never wish to stray!'*

Keep the garment in your possession
for at least seven days. After that,
you can leave it somewhere for him
or her to find.

If you ever get a *frisson* of
discomfort with regards to potential
infidelity, dab a little of the oil onto
yourself. If they seem to be straying
anyway, bring those mental barriers
down around you again. Repeat as
necessary, but be sensible.
Sometimes the tides change, and
it is best to let go.

CHAKRIC NUTRIENTS

Food can be used for psychic purposes, to enhance visualisation and strengthen the astral body through their colours. Green foods strengthen the heart chakra (or energy point), red foods aid with determination, and yellow/orange foods such squash and mango help to build up emotional strength and independence, courtesy of the solar plexus chakra. Meals can be concocted to aid any spell or visualisation.

PSYCHIC BEVERAGES

The liquids we put into our bodies are also psychically relevant. Water purifies on all levels. Tea and coffee aid with determination and creativity. Red wine is symbolic of the blood of Life. Herb teas, of course, have numerous different properties. Colour is as important as content, especially in visualisation.

Thus, any solid or liquid is potentially a spell.

FORTIFIED CIDER

Because of its deep golden colour
and its origin of apples, cider is
a great carrier for health
visualisations. Only one small
glass per spell, mind!

Take a modest measure of sweet
cider. Drop a tiger's eye gem into it.
Light a yellow candle, and place it
behind the glass, so that you can see
the flame through the liquid.

Envisage healthful light streaming
into the candle, its focus point the
flame. As the flame illuminates the
golden-orange brew, visualise this
vibrancy being transferred into the
cider. Keep this visualisation up for
as long as you are able.

When finished, slowly drink the cider (beware the tiger's eye!). With each sip, feel light and health entering your body, driving out any unwanted 'dark' patches. By the end of the glass, your astral body should be literally glowing with health!

TROUBLESOME WORKMATE OR BOSS

If you are being dealt with unfairly by a peer or authority figure, work on a Thursday when the moon is waxing. A little Libra incense (available from most good New Age shops) will also help with this.

Light a purple candle, and envisage the Scales of Justice. In one pan visualise yourself, in the other the person(s) concerned. See how the scales are weighted unfairly? (They should be. If not, you might wish to reconsider your position!)

So too must everybody else. Mentally magnify the scales, and, if you can, visualise the relevant external parties gawping in outrage.

Now appeal to the universal Justice-makers, such as Jupiter and Maat, to tip the scales back to a position fair to you. Keep performing this exercise until the pans are in balance again.

TO GAIN EMPLOYMENT

Take a small citrine stone (often available polished from New Age stores) and concentrate orange light into it. Embalming it with a little orange oil may well aid this process. The citrine is known to enhance confidence, and orange helps with the organisational skill, self-control and focus required at interviews. Even when writing letters of application, this simple charm can be used, either kept at your side or in a pocket, etc. If you can find a piece of citrine through which a chain (or even bootlace) can be strung, all the better — this will enable you to wear it about your neck and thus have its influence close to your chakras!

FAST MONEY

As with any augmenting spell, the following is best worked with a waxing moon. Take a gold, red or green candle, and anoint it with a little clove oil. As you light the wick, imagine money being attracted to you. Be sure to add the proviso that this is through no harm to yourself, or anybody else! (Insurance money, for example, could be one of the ways for this spell to backfire if the ground rules are not set!) Persistence pays off in magick, so if you can find the time and inspiration to repeat this every day until the full moon, all the better. Starting on a Thursday will kick-start the process.

HIGHER SELF

It can be difficult to stay attuned to one's higher purpose in this work-a-day world, even when living with strong metaphysical beliefs.

Creating a small 'sacred space' to visit every day is an effective way to counteract the mundane. This does not have to be physical, but if you have room for an altar in a space conducive to meditation, all the better. You can embellish this as you progress, starting with objects of significance in the past, and progressing on to those relevant at present.

Alternatively, you can create an 'Astral Temple' (see eponymous spell p.66).

Visit your space as often as you can. Use it to attune your physical manifestation with your higher purpose. Three points to dwell on are: What am I achieving in this incarnation? What am I meant to learn from my life to date — what are the recurring themes? How can I follow my inner calling in order to make my life happy, creative and beneficial to others?

ASTRAL TEMPLE

Recall a place that you loved, or imagine an environment that seems magickal to you. Envisage it very strongly.

Now put something there. You might like to plant a shrub or tree, or to mentally place a beloved object on the spot.

Return to your sanctuary the following day. Look at whatever you placed there. If it is still as new, or is flourishing, this is a good 'place' for you to come. If not, try again until you are happy with the results.

Whenever you wish to cast a spell or
ponder the higher aspects of life,
see and feel yourself in this place,
your astral temple.

The connections to your sacred
space will grow as you do. You will
soon find that your 'imaginary'
hideout has a life of its own.

KINDLY EXORCISM

If you are being blighted by a troublesome spirit, do not follow the conventional exorcism techniques, unless it is truly evil (which is highly unlikely). This causes great distress to a spirit that is obviously already undergoing difficulties.

Instead, try to get a sense of its personality. Then construct an appealing mental landscape for it to inhabit. Behind this, envisage the Light of cosmic compassion and progression.

Invite the spirit into your landscape.
The more vivid and appealing this is,
the better.

When the spirit has 'moved into'
your appealing landscape,
concentrate on the Light, asking
the Powers that Be to take the
entity on.

ANCESTRAL WORSHIP

As incarnating souls, we gravitate towards families who will teach us what we need to know. Even if our immediate family does not seem spiritually relevant (in an obvious sense), we frequently discover predecessors with the same interests and spiritual urges. It is possible to connect with those 'familiar' spirits who are willing.

Sitting quietly, carry a line of light that starts at your forehead, backwards from the present moment through your life, with all its major events (in reverse order), until you reach the point of your birth.

Now repeat the process with the parent whose bloodline you are choosing to study. See him or her retreating in time until the point of their conception. Repeat with a grandparent, until your thread reaches the ancestor you wish to contact.

Envisage the light connecting you both, and send your thoughts down it, as if it were a phone line. With any luck, you should receive an answer.

ANY PURPOSE SPELL

The technique of 'sigilisation' was brought into modern magick by Austin Osman Spare. It is a simple and effective way to imprint the subconscious with a desired result.

Create a sentence that summarises what you want. Be clear, and aim for one thing at a time. Write it down, and take the first letter of every word. If any letters are repeated, reduce them to just one.

Take all the letters and create a 'monogram' of them. It's fine for lines to overlap or be written backwards.

You should end up with a magickal-looking but indecipherable symbol.

When you are emotionally charged up, stare at it. No need to recall its intent — your subconscious will do that for you. The greater the energy directed at it, the bigger the end result.

BLESSING A PET THAT HAS PASSED OVER

It is heartbreaking to lose a beloved pet, even when we believe in the afterlife. Sometimes we do not get the chance to say goodbye, which makes our loss feel even worse.

Take a treat that was favoured by your pet, and place it before a blue votive candle along with a photo of you both together.

Light the candle, gently thinking the animal's name. When your pet appears (dogs are better at this than cats), welcome it, and mentally 'give' it the treat. Thank it for your time together — elaborate as wished.

Explain that you realise it was your pet's time to go (otherwise the pet may not be able to move on), and wish it joyous new-found independence.

When you are finished, blow out the candle and bury the treat in your garden, or, if you have none, leave it in a place favoured by your beloved pet. They would not begrudge another animal taking their treat, now.

SIXTH SENSES

The image produced by Kahlil Gibran in *The Prophet*, of a palm with an eye in it, can be employed in visualisation to enhance the sixth sense.

With your eyes closed, sit opposite the person or object you wish to psychically perceive, your palms open to them/it. Envisage eyes in the palms' centre, emitting rays of emerald and violet light towards your subject.

Relax, and let your intuition flow.

CHILL OUT, YOU!

To cause another person to chill out, try to procure a sample of their handwriting, preferably produced when they are irate. Alternatively, draw a small picture of them as they appear when angry.

Fold the paper up as tightly as possible, and wrap in a little cling-film, saying:

'Keep the fires of wrath from spilling; To calméd be I spell you willing!'

Place in an ice tray, and pop that into the freezer.

AUTO CHILL OUT

I use this technique whenever the humdrum aspects of life and relationships are getting in the way of spiritual integrity. It may be performed anywhere.

Imagine yourself sitting in a snowy mountain range such as the Himalayas. It is night, and a full moon shines brightly above. You are completely alone. In your hands is a crystal ball. In it are images of your life's actions. Watch the most relevant scenes play themselves out before you.

Now imagine that your life has ended, and all that is in the crystal ball is all you have achieved in that incarnation.

Assess what it is that you wish you had done differently.

When ready, 'transfer' yourself into the crystal ball, and put into action the principles which you could see, with your 'overview', were required to make your life worthwhile.

TO ATTRACT AMIABLE SPIRITS FROM THE OTHER SIDE

Voodoo altars often feature cups of whisky and rum to attract and thank spirits helpful to the practitioner. Any offering will bring spirits to whom such a gift appeals.

So, decide the sort of spirits whose company you would enjoy, and make them gifts of a suitable nature; perhaps a sweet cake or something that, to you, represents enduring friendship.

On the night of a new moon, light a candle of pale green, and another of pale pink. Place them on your altar

or a small table, along with a stick
of sweet-smelling incense such as
rose or jasmine. Say:

*'Accept these gifts, and
Blesséd Be: Happy spirits, come
to me.'*

Place your welcome gifts with the
candles. When you perceive a spirit
who suits your purpose, say:

'Merry Meet.'

When you wish them to depart (and
return), say:

*'Merry Part; and Merry
Meet again.'*

TO ATTRACT AMIABLE PEOPLE

On the night of a new moon, light two candles, one of dark green, and one of vibrant pink. Light a sweet-smelling joss stick such as gardenia or rose. Take a photograph of yourself with your best friends, and hold it out to the moon. Turn it over three times, saying:

'Power of friendship, others see: Return to me by the power of Three!'

PICK ME!

If you wish to be selected for a particular endeavour, take a red candle and, on the night of a full moon, anoint it with clove oil. Light the candle and think of everything that befits you to this post. Envisage yourself surrounded by vibrant red-orange light, like that created by the candle, and crackling with the 'electricity' of your enthusiasm.

Recreate this light whenever you think of yourself in a position to be picked. If this involves a face-to-face encounter, dab yourself with a little clove oil on the day.

TO QUIETEN A GOSSIP

Perform this spell when the
moon is waning.

To bind a malicious tongue, write
down the full initials of its owner.
Eliminate any repeated letters.
Translate into your favourite runic or
magickal script. Make a monogram
of these characters, so that you are
left with a figure that represents
them to you. Carve this onto a small
piece of wood, saying

*'Though thy tongue was once so
free, now it's wooden:
One, Two, Three.'*

With each number, carve a line
through the name.

Every time you hear or think of this
person gossiping, visualise your runic
monogram on their tongue.

TO QUELL A TROUBLEMAKER

Use this spell to neutralise a pesky influence without causing harm to its perpetrator.

On the night of, or after, a full moon, take a small black candle. Hold it in your hands and think of all the trouble caused by the relevant party. The candle represents it.

Using a needle, carve the initials of the troublemaker into the candle. Now burn it, thinking of the trouble diminishing.

Repeat every night of the waning moon, until the candle is spent. Take the tiny bit of wax and wick that remains, and stick the needle through it. Wrap needle and spent candle in a piece of white silk, and bury it in a graveyard.

DRYADIC COMFORT

Trees are one of nature's most wondrous gifts, as most people would agree. Occasionally, however, vandals rip down striplings or take branches from older trees, causing distress to the tree and the community alike.

To comfort the tree-spirit, sit down close to it, perhaps holding a branch or leaf in your hands, and attune yourself to the nature Deva (or guardian entity) in charge. This can be done by reaching out your mind and 'asking' to connect. A slight shimmer or your intuition will tell you when you are being perceived by the spirit of the tree.

Tell the spirit how much you enjoyed it, and that you wish to donate some of your energy to help it heal. If the tree is completely ruined (as were two young blossoming cherries in my mother's village recently), thank it for the pleasure it gave you, and send energy anyway. The organic manifestation is dead, but the nature Deva is not.

PROTECTING A CHILD

Actions speak louder than spells
when it comes to child protection,
but this may be used to enhance
whatever you are doing on the
material plane.

Take a photo of the child, or a lock
of his or her hair. Place it on a small
square of soft yellow cloth.

Hold a shiny new penny up to the
sun, and say:

*'One in a hundred, a hundred
in one; Give health and
protection, Spiritual Sun!'*

Place this with the photo or hair.

Now add three comfrey leaves to
the contents, and send a ray of love

and protection into the ingredients.
Tie with a white ribbon so that it
becomes a pouch.

Hide this in the room of the child.

MAGICKAL
ENHANCEMENT

Any focused ritual repeated often
enough will boost your magickal
powers. Intent is everything in
magick. Use your intuition! A simple
example is working with the waxing
moon, burning a purple votive
candle every evening, and
concentrating on the
accumulation of Universal Energy,
which may be used for
any purpose.

JEALOUSY-RIDDER: SELF

Work with the waning moon.

Take a black candle and anoint, from centre to tip in both directions, with cypress or mimosa oil. Burn a patchouli scented joss-stick as you work.

Think about all the things you feel jealous about. Invest the candle with these energies, but don't light it! You've made the effort to break the effects of your self-pollution on the earth plane; now you're going to break it on the astral too.

Place the candle over a piece of green silk.

Thinking of all the reasons to rid yourself of this plague, snap the candle. Now break it up in whatever way and as much as you desire.

Collect all the pieces in the silk, and tie with a white ribbon.

Chuck it wherever you chuck the other things you no longer wish to possess. Complete the effect by taking a purification bath in energised salt water.

JEALOUSY-RIDDER: OTHERS

On a night of the waning moon (nearest to the full moon is best), take a black or purple candle and anoint with cypress oil from centre to tip and centre to base, thinking of how the cleansing aroma of the cypress is already freshening the perceptions of your 'rival'.

Now take three dried rose petals and, using tweezers, hold them one by one in the flame. This is symbolic of your friendship and patience sweetening the atmosphere.

Project all the positive, healing energy you can at the person, and send as much love to them as you can muster.

Either burn the candle down to its base, working on consecutive nights (no need to use petals and leaves again, unless you wish to), or burn it all now. Wrap any remains with a few comfrey leaves and bury (use a biodegradable wrapper!).

GARTER OF VENUS

Every witch knows how to use
a garter to her best advantage.
Traditionally, they were male
vestments, as worn by the Knights
of that order, but they have become
a female province.

Take one ready-made garter, or,
for extra energy, create one yourself
out of three ribbons. Tie the ribbons
at the top and plait loosely
nine times.

On a Friday, when the moon is
waxing or full, take your garter with
you into the moonlight. Hold it up to
the Goddess, and contemplate the

magickal enchantment it will
produce when wrapped around your
thigh. Ask for the powers of
seduction known to so many
goddesses, ancient and modern,
to be invested into your
magickal apparel.

Wear it on your next date.

SAGE SPELL

The American Indians used bunches of sage to cleanse the atmosphere of evil influences. This works, but the smell can be rather overpowering. Work at the new moon, and keep the windows open. Move from room to room with your burning sage bundle (widely available from New Age stores), and as you waft the cleansing incense about, envisage all negative entities and atmospheres fleeing through the open windows, or being dissolved by the astringent smoke.

Finally, banish the remains by waving them out. When the smoke has departed, and just a faint scent remains, close your windows and mentally seal them and the doors from unwanted beings and atmospheres.

COUPLE ATTUNEMENT

To attune spiritually and psychically
with your partner, sit cross-legged,
face-to-face. You are going to
utilise the chakra system; that is,
the seven major energy points of the
body and aura which run from the
base of the spine to the crown
of the head.

Starting at the base chakra, imagine
a line of light connecting you both.
Do the same with the intestinal
chakra. Continue up through the
solar plexus, heart, throat, third eye
and finally the crown chakras.

Now envisage all seven major energy
centres linked.

Whenever you and your partner feel you are becoming separated, for whatever reason, repeat this process. You will soon find that you are never truly 'apart'.

INTUITION

If you feel yourself to be lacking in the intuition department (hopefully you are insightful enough to know!), use Mondays to meditate upon the moon. Even just a small time spent contemplating the silver orb before you sleep will help. You will soon find yourself becoming attuned to the psychic wavelengths traditionally associated with that planet.

TO STRENGTHEN
A LONG-DISTANCE
FRIENDSHIP

If you have a close and trusted
friend who has moved abroad or to
a far-flung town, you will find your
time together even more precious.
Buy an A3 notepad, and, when
together, light an orange candle
over it. Together, say:

*'Merry Meet and Merry Part:
Before I go, my heart I'll
show.'*

Now, each make a dated entry in
the book. Decide on a 'keeper' of
the Journal.

Every time you meet, repeat the incantation, and then use the pages to explore your progress and thoughts since you last met.

I've been doing this with a witchy friend for years now, and what started off as a regular diary has become a fascinating and enlightening Book of Shadows. (Many witches record their spells in a Book of Shadows.)

Ritual and honesty cannot fail to enhance a friendship.

TO ENHANCE A CLOSE FRIENDSHIP

Buy a pack of Tarot cards with your best friend. Pick a set that you both feel is appropriate to your joint energy.

Sitting face-to-face, take turns to shuffle the cards. Concentrate on the energy you produce together as you do so. This is aided by envisaging the light emanating from each of you, its cohesion, and its effect on the Tarot.

Wrap the pack in a black silk scarf.

Whenever either of you is confused or distressed, or simply in need of some guidance, get the other one to read from the pack. If you need a book at first, don't worry — it takes years to really learn the cards.

After a few tries with this, you will find both your friendship and your psychic sensitivity regarding your friend greatly enhanced.

LINES OF LIGHT

Use this spell to pick out people who can benefit you, whatever your endeavour.

On a Thursday when the moon is waxing, light an orange candle, and think of the type of people you wish to attract, and how you will be of mutual benefit. Say:

*'If they be of use to me,
Lines of vibrant light I'll see.'*

When you find yourself placed before people of potential relevance, look above their heads with your intuition switched on.

Those with lines of light above them are — you got it! — the people it is worth expending your energy on.

PSYCHOMANCY SPELL

Many psychics are able to pick up details of people and places from objects they handle. To develop this art, take some rock salt, and hold it up to the moon when visible, saying:

*Purify my hands and mind:
In what I touch, the truth
I'll find.*

Dissolve the salt in hot mineral water, and wash your hands in it, whilst visualising bright white light purifying and imbuing your being, particularly your hands.

Before you touch any object you wish to receive information from, visualise this light, and repeat the process if possible.

NULLIFYING NEGATIVITY

To diminish unwanted emotions, take a small black candle and mentally imbue it with your wrath / jealousy / insecurity / negativity. As it burns, envisage these life-hindering energies dissipating into raw, pure silver energy. Mentally re-absorb the energy, now cleansed, and resolve to use it constructively. Be warned; its power is now redoubled!

WOW!

To make your impact on a potential lover, look straight into their eyes (by candle- or firelight is best, but any intimate situation will do), and envisage a fishing line, complete with hook, coming out of your pupils, into theirs, and down into their gut. Do your utmost to connect psychically.

Every time you think good thoughts about them, remember that line, and send all of your positive, sparkly energy down it.

You should prove gut-wrenchingly irresistible to them.

DIVINATION BY TV

This technique was propounded in
its original form by The Temple of
Psychick Youth in the 1990s.

Sit in contemplation for a while, in
as much silence as is possible in this
day and age. Attune yourself to the
Universe.

Now think of all the networks of
communication that span the world
— the psychic and spiritual, the
electronic and technological.
Meditate on the fact that everything
we chose to perceive is of
significance to us.

Concentrate on a question you would like to ask, or a theme that is of particular relevance to you at present. Ask the Universe to give you an accurate response.

Now, turn on the television (or radio) and hop channels swiftly. The images, words and phrases received are your answers.

FOLLOW ME, BOY

When neither the sun nor the moon
is visible, place four drops of vervain
oil in a mortar with three mistletoe
berries, and crush. Visualise the
symbol of Venus (♀) filling the sky
as you do so, sending rays of pinkish
silver light into your potion,
and you.

If you are after a particular man,
say:

*'If none it harm,
enhance my charm,'*

imagining him attached to you by
seven strong but beautiful lines of
pinkish silver light. Now visualise
him, still attached, scintillated
by you.

If you are simply looking for fun,
imagine yourself shining like the
symbol, your rays going out in
many directions.

When you feel the mistletoe mush
is charged, apply immediately to
your pulse points, or, if you wish to
delay the effects of your spell, place
it in a dark glass container and use
when required.

Now say:

Follow me, boy,

and enjoy.

FOLLOW ME, GIRL

Under a full moon, and preferably
when Venus is visible, slowly anoint
a dried vanilla pod with seven drops
of vanilla oil. Place in a small bag
with five red rose petals. As you
place the petals in the pouch,
imagine yourself 'bagging' the girl.
(Or a girl who matches your
specifications.)

Now say:

*'An' none it harm,
Enhance this charm.'*

Sprinkle the vanilla pod and rose
petals with ten pinches of
cinnamon, saying:

'For lust and trust, follow me, girl! For leisure and pleasure, follow me, girl! For all that you treasure, follow me girl!'

(Naive verses create more effective magick, precisely because of their childlike simplicity.) When you have visualised the object of your desire smilingly following you, tie the pouch with a green ribbon.

Carry your charm on a string around your neck (under your clothes, of course!) or in an upper pocket. When you wish to activate it, tap seven times, and smile.

If she is willing on a higher level, the girl will follow.

SPIRIT FLIGHT

Need a break? Why not get out of your body?! This technique may take practice, or it may occur spontaneously, but either way it results in the ultimate nocturnal holiday — astral travel.

Take one purple candle and, from centre to base and centre to tip, anoint with wormwood oil. If you cannot get this, ginseng oil or balsam will suffice.

When the candle is charged, light it. Just before bed is best, but any time will do. Sit cross-legged before it (in the lotus posture if possible), spine straight. Shut your eyes, but still see the candle — at the level of your third eye, between and slightly above the eyebrows. Now visualise yourself above it. Rise as high as you can. When you are ready, return to your body, open your eyes, and extinguish the flame.

You need only perform this for a few minutes every day; the key is the regularity of your desire to exit your body.

Soon, your spirit will fly at night.

GROUNDING SPELL

There are times when consciousness seems like a kite stuck between conflicting currents, and needs to be reeled in and grounded. If you are unable to concentrate owing to others, or because of your own thoughts and emotions, this simple spell is for you.

Take a pinch of soil and a pinch of salt, and place them with a small stone in a pouch. Once done, say (or think loudly) the following words:

'Salt of Salt. Earth of Earth,'

stamping on the ground with each syllable.

Whenever you need to be grounded, squeeze the bag in the palm of your

hand, and repeat the words
mentally ten times over. This also
works to diminish negative
influences and to counteract psychic
attack, should you be unfortunate
enough to undergo it.

HOLISTIC BOOST

For self-confidence, carry a sprig of
fresh rosemary about your person.
When you need strength and
refreshment, rub it between your
thumb and forefinger. This is also a
good remedy for headaches,
neuralgia, hyper-tension and
unwanted influences.

LAUNCHING A PROJECT

Buy a flowering potted geranium. Procure a picture or statue of one of the following: Ganesha, Laxmi, Apollo, St Peter, or any other deity/intercessor you like whose auspices are good in a business sense (one may think laterally — Apollo's archery guarantees far-sightedness and precision work, for example, while his solar qualities bring propitious circumstances).

Place the plant before the godform, saying (or thinking):

'May my venture prosper and flourish like the flowers of this plant.'

Imagine golden light streaming from above the head of your celestial business partner, through their body, and radiating into you.

Now light a stick of incense as a thank-you, placing it in the soil of your plant to burn. Repeat as required.

We cannot expect a potted plant to keep its flowers forever, so, to avoid expiry vibes, remove as soon as the flowers begin to wither. Replacement blooms are best in yellow and orange to red.

INVOKING THE GODDESS

Personified female energies of the Creative Intelligence may be invoked for specific purposes. Examples are:

* The Egyptian Isis, for magick, fertility, love

* Persephone, Demeter's daughter in Greek mythology, for transcending unwanted situations

* Hera, Zeus' Olympian wife, for a pro-active approach to setting errant partners straight

＊Nephthys, sister of Isis, for inner strength and overcoming grief

A knowledge of mythology and its archetypes brings great rewards in magick, allowing the practitioner to link with established psychological and subconscious patterns.

INVOKING THE GODS

In addition to goddesses, personified godforms can be invoked with powerful effect. Some examples are:

* Pan, the goat-footed god of Greek mythology, to break a deadlock, halt complacency, liberate sexuality

* The Egyptian Osiris, to emerge smiling from a situation of enmity

* Horus, son of Isis and Osiris, for balance, communication skills

* Thoth, the Egyptian scribe and magickian, for academe/learning

∗Odin, the Norse god who suffered to attain the runes for mankind, to help attune to a greater good

LIGHT OF INTUITION

At the full moon, take an overview of your life. Are you heading in the direction you want to? Is your life-path fulfilling, progressive and fun? Meditating by the light of the lunar orb, particularly with the aid of a trusty Tarot pack and a Book of Shadows (your Magickal Diary), you will gain enhanced perspective and insight regarding your life's true purpose.

TALISMANIC MAGIC

There are talismans available
to suit any religious proclivity.
A protective rune worn about the
neck for those who relate to the
Norse gods, a hieroglyph cast in
precious metal or a trusty scarab for
those who prefer Egyptian lore. An
equilateral cross confers balance to
a Qabalist. Pick your talisman to suit
your inclinations and purpose.

When you find or make it, direct
brilliant blue light at it, and say:

*'Protection to the left of me,
protection to the right of me,
before me, behind me, over
me, under me. So mote it be.'*

Charge your talisman with extra
energy to meet particular
challenges, as they occur.

TOOLS OF
ENCHANTMENT

Some of the most psychically
effective equipment is the simplest.
A cut crystal hung in the window,
for example, will shift stale energy
with spectrum colour-magick. Wind
chimes also add magick to the
atmosphere and keep negative
entities at bay. Both produce
harmony in a room
or household.

AROMATIC AID

A couple of drops of essential oil in a burner or in the bath will change your day. Choose:

* Sandalwood for emotional warmth and magick

* Ylang Ylang and Geranium for ideas and inspiration

* Lavender for mental clarity

* Frankincense to encourage prosperity

* Orange for friendship and happiness

APHRODITE'S REFRESHER

To re-invoke love in a relationship, take alternate sips with your partner from a silver chalice (or a chalice-shaped glass) containing fresh strawberry juice and some halves of the fruit, topped up with champagne. You will soon find good vibrations flowing between you again.

ROSE-TINTED BATH

To engender love and compassion
betwixt yourself and those who may
not make it easy:

Soak a lump of rose quartz and
a polished pebble of the same rock
in cold water at the bottom of the
bath for at least an hour, then
remove the gemstones, add hot
water and sprinkle six drops of
rose oil in the loving brew. Get in,
envisaging the water glowing pink
and your/their negativity
evaporating. Think of interacting in
perfect harmony. Relax and enjoy.

When you emerge, continue to visualise yourself glowing with this pink energy. Take the smaller of the rose quartz, hold it, and transfer your new colour into it. It may help to rub it with a little rose oil.

Put the pebble in your pocket when you go out, and hold it in your hand whenever the situation arises. 'See' the pink light emanating from the gemstone and recharging you with positivity.

You may like to attempt to transfer this to the other party too.

DIVINE NOURISHMENT

Light a yellow candle with a request
for health and prosperity. Envisage
nourishing golden light flowing from
the Universe into the focus of the
flame, then into you. When you are
sated and glowing, extinguish the
flame, and feel yourself emanating
its light from every pore. When
depleted, repeat.

ENLIVENING THE CHAKRAS

Light a small rainbow candle,
and as it burns, concentrate on each
chakra (or energy centre) in turn,
as follows:

*Red — Base chakra

*Orange — Intestinal chakra

*Yellow — Solar Plexus chakra

*Green — Heart chakra

*Blue — Throat chakra

*Purple — Third Eye chakra

*Flame — Crown chakra

You will soon feel psychically
refreshed, and ready for
magick on any plane.

CHAKRA-CLEANSER

Keep a quartz crystal in the water container you use the most. The longer the crystal is in soak, the stronger the purifying properties of the water will be. As you drink the crystal water, feel it cleansing your subtle and physical bodies, brightening and energising your chakras.

YESODIC BOOST

For creative inspiration, imagine you are standing on the snow-capped peak of a purple mountain beneath a harvest moon. Feel the vibrational essence of inner life all around you; allow it to enter your system through the crown of your head and between your eyebrows. When you are ready, return to everyday life. You should find your imaginative capacities greatly enhanced.

KARMIC CALMER

If you are angry and do not wish to be, remove yourself from the situation of emotional toxicity, then breathe in white light and envisage red light exiting your body as you exhale. As you calm down, it grows pinker and paler. When the light you exhale is white, it is safe to re-enter the fray, resolving this time to keep your cool.

NO PAIN, NO GAIN

Remember that every discomfort
you undergo and every problem you
encounter is nullifying your personal
karma. Thus nothing, however
seemingly pointless, is without
its purpose.

Realise that you deserve the best in
life because you will use it well, and
to the benefit of all.

PSYCHIC ENHANCEMENT

Get a friend to put a mystery object into a box. With your eyes closed, concentrate on your third-eye area, and imagine it bathed in violet light. Slowly 'open' this eye, and try to 'see' what is in the box. Do not think; use intuition only.

For lateral spells and visualisations to increase psychic ability, intuition and to get to the bottom of emotional depths, work on a Monday. Use Jasmine oil or incense, or anything which to you is lunar/ethereal. Suitable props include silver, moonstone, pearl, quartz crystal and milk.

TRAVEL TONIC

Worried about a journey? A couple
of drops of comfrey oil on a blue silk
square will help keep fear and peril
at bay. A bath beforehand
containing a few comfrey leaves will
also soothe troubled nerves.

Gods who specialise in helping
travellers include the Greek god
Hermes, and Anubis, the Egyptian
jackal-headed god, so concentrating
on them and asking that you be
guided safely to your destination
may also help.

GEBURIC DEFENCES

To overcome enmity and increase
personal power, work on a Tuesday.
Cedar and tobacco are appropriate
fragrances; ritual paraphernalia can
be ferrous, red and symbolically
militarian; magickal daggers and
swords, for example (though these
are never used to harm, but to
channel energy).

This is a good day to bless a ritual
sword, if you have one. If not,
try this:

Visualise all of your determination
and will to succeed as a long sharp
sword. Envisage the hilt too,

the metal of which it is made, and any other suitable details. Concentrate on it until it is completely 'solid' in your mind.

Every time you have a battle on your hands, envisage your sword hacking away at any obstacles.

'Clean' your sword regularly, by imagining brilliant light flowing through it and dissolving all pollutants. You should find your determination and ability to succeed greatly enhanced.

THE CELTIC TREE CALENDAR

Appealing to those of us with a penchant for nature-spirits, this ancient system catalogues the seasons and their corresponding trees, moods and energies. Studying the trees concerned deeply enhances perception of each month. Epic poems such as *The Battle of the Trees* amply describe their traits, as perceived in Bardic lore and analysed in Robert Graves' *The White Goddess*, a literary touchstone in every witch and poet's library.

*Beth (Birch): 24 December— 20 January

*Luis (Rowan): 21 January— 17 February

*Nion (Ash): 18 February—17 March

*Fearn (Alder): 18 March—14 April

*Saille (Willow): 15 April—12 May

*Uath (Hawthorn):13 May—9 June

*Duir (Oak): 10 June—7July

*Tinne (Holly): 8 July—4 August

*Coll (Hazel): 5 August—
1 September

*Muin (Vine): 2 September—
29 September

*Gort (Ivy): 30 September—
27 October

*Ngetal (Reed): 28 October—
24 November

*Ruis (Elder): 25 November—
22 December

FOR MENTAL ALERTNESS

For issues of academe, communication, ritual and business scenarios, Wednesday gives the optimum influences. Lavender is mentally bracing and eight drops burned in a censer will work wonders. Shower rather than bathe. Use the caduceus symbol (two snakes wrapped around a staff) to help focus your mind.

QUICK BOOSTER VISUALISATION

Lacking in energy? Go outside, preferably somewhere fresh and in sunlight, and take several deep lungfuls of the air.

As you inhale, envisage the bright prana, or life-energy, entering your lungs until they glow. Now 'see' that light being absorbed through them into your bloodstream, coursing round your body, bringing refreshment and clean energy to your system.

RITUAL TOOLS

Candles and incense are important ritual tools, as they can hone the mind to a very specific goal if selected appropriately. Other classical witch's tools include the athame, or black-handled knife, the boline, which is white-handled and curved and used for harvesting herbs, the chalice, and sometimes the ritual sword, for channelling energy. None of these implements is ever used to cause harm, but they are all helpful symbols.

Real magick happens when a mind interacts with the Universe and impresses its Will on the subtle energies that determine our lives.

The essential ritual tools for any witch are therefore the ability to visualise creatively, and the determination and enthusiasm to succeed.

URBANE INSPIRATION

If you've got the urban blues, a (carefully tended) midnight bonfire will chill and thrill the harassed Pagan within. Or wax lyrical by candlelight with friends and children in Druidic style, expelling the smog from the lungs of the city-clogged Bard with saga and song.

THOUGHTFORMS

Remember that whatever you imagine becomes real on the astral plane. If envisaged frequently enough, it may take on a form and energy of its own. Positive thoughts are of infinitely more benefit than negative ones, which pollute the aura and may cause all kinds of unpleasantness. Create a repository of strength by establishing an astral container (in whatever form you wish) for happiness and inspiration, when you feel it. This can become a point of psychic pilgrimage, helping to maintain equilibrium when the chips are down.

AN AROMATIC ANTIDOTE TO CIGARETTE CRAVINGS

Lavender oil can help you quit smoking. A room full of evaporated lavender is healthier and more fragrant than toxic tobacco, and it really helps diminish the urge. Try it!

THE POWER OF CONVICTION

If you really want something (within reason), imagine that you already have it. The surer you are that it 'belongs' to you, the more magnetic will you become to that object/situation. The stronger your visualisation and imagining that you have it, the surer you are of success. So choose your desires carefully!

DIVINATION BY FIRE, AIR AND EARTH

For powers of prophecy, burn a
miniature Fire of Azrael (as a
divining fire is known) by using
cedar chips, juniper and sandalwood
on a charcoal disc. What can you see
in the flames and what do the
shapes in the smoke symbolise
to you?

TO ATTRACT THE APPLE OF YOUR EYE

Unrequited love? Eat a red apple in the vicinity of your beloved, then plant the core during a waxing moon, saying:

'Seeds of love, grow strong and blossom.'

Visualise the other person's love taking root in you, just as the apple's seeds take root in the earth. Imagine their growth and pleasure being sustained by your interaction as the apple was eaten. Soon the Venusian allure will take effect.

PSYCHIC
SELF-PROTECTION

For psychic self-protection, envisage
yourself at the centre of a tongue of
blue fire. Within this psychic flame
you are inviolate. Approaching
detrimental forces are instantly
incinerated, but beneficial ones are
absorbed and add lustre to your
light. The latter, burning super-
bright, sends shades and shadows
packing in the Astral realms. Thus
you are at once protected and a
living luminary.

GENTLE EXORCISM

To rid a home or room of unwanted influences, place some salt in water in the North-West of a room, incense in the East and a bell and candle in the South. Walking clockwise, ring the bell, flick a little of the salt water and waft the incense, saying:

'Sorrows past be gone.
Love and light stay long.'

ASTRAL ARMOUR

(See also Psychic Self-Protection
on p. 155)

For double psychic protection in times
of crisis, imagine that the aura-flame
is a fluid suit of armour. You can check
its durability by mentally 'bouncing'
an attack off its surface. 'See' and
feel the virulent words / emotions
/thoughts rebounding from it and
returning to sender. (If you are feeling
kind, you could visualise them being
earthed.) Know that your suit of astral
armour will let none of the slings and
arrows of outrageous colleagues
/partners / family members in,
and that your callousness to their
entreaty or attack is complete.

GLIMPSING THE
VANISHING PEOPLE

Don't believe in faeries? On Beltane
or Midsummer's Eve at twilight, sit in
a natural surround and entwine seven
inches of red ribbon with two ribbons
of green about the stem of an oak,
hawthorn or spindle-tree. As you do so,
sense the elemental interest your act
engenders. Soon you should perceive
the peer of elfin eyes on your
enterprise, tingling in your fingers and
tip-tapping at your sensitive spine.
Allow your intuition to roam the
subtler plane, and you will not be
blinkered by disbelief again.

The easiest way to
ruin magickal work
is to talk about it,
so Know, Will, Dare,
and BE SILENT!